# They Were Different

Neil J. Kenney

Alpha Editions

This edition published in 2023

ISBN : 9789357949682

Design and Setting By
**Alpha Editions**
www.alphaedis.com
Email - info@alphaedis.com

As per information held with us this book is in Public Domain.
This book is a reproduction of an important historical work. Alpha Editions uses the best technology to reproduce historical work in the same manner it was first published to preserve its original nature. Any marks or number seen are left intentionally to preserve its true form.

# Contents

THEY WERE DIFFERENT ............................................. - 1 -
BY NEIL J. KENNEY ..................................................... - 1 -

# THEY WERE DIFFERENT

## BY NEIL J. KENNEY

*As secretary, receptionist and general nursemaid to them I took it upon myself to dig back through the news files and get enough clips to tell their history from birth until they opened the school. You've all read it so there's no need to go into details about their strange life and still stranger birth. Nor their magnificent education or still more magnificent gifts. It's true, every bit of it; their telepathic and ESPing powers WORKED. They were the only births like them to survive to maturity and beyond.*

*During the last contact I had with them (I was their first and most advanced pupil) it came as pure inspiration to take down their transmissions in the special short, shorthand we developed for use among the pupils and ourselves. What follows may be added to the story told by the news clips, differing only in person. I have added nothing in translation of the notes, leaving the narrative as disjointed as they gave it. The events are as they transmitted them, as they lived them. I was in contact with them until—but read, and when you're through reading do as I do every night.*

*Pray.*

*And hope—for mankind.*

Well, Kitten, it seems impossible that three grand, successful years of work could end so suddenly with us lying in a ditch or anticipating, ESPwise, an occasional bullet fired from the guns of friends but there it is. God, what a complicated being this so-called modern man is! He seems to be born cloaked with complexities which get even more complex as he grows. No wonder he has been so long on the road, being engaged in a continual battle between ethics and emotions as he has.

So here we are, the bridge, the first rungs of a ladder leading to a new and delightful plane of existence for all mankind, wallowing in the mud of an irrigation ditch instead of glorying in the divine world of the mind. If we can but make them see! Maybe the professors were right when they told us to teach under the protection of the university instead of hardheadedly going out on our own.

Princess, do you remember Lucille? She was our best pupil, after you, of course. She's the one who turned over the stone that freed our personal gremlin. Oh, it's not really her fault, though she did break our one and only cardinal rule by bringing in an outsider herself instead of leaving such choices to us. Actually the fault was ours because—well, who knows? That wonderful control we practiced for so many years slipped, no matter the reason. It was just one of those inexplicably foolish things people will do when they think they're in love. Guess we thought we could save her some embarrassment or some such thing.

You had just left on a long vacation when *that* one showed up. He was the man that Lucille brought up with her as a prospective pupil, the one that—one wing of them is closing in on us now, Kitten. We'll have to try for the swamp ahead of us. We'll have to lose them for a while if we want time to figure a way out, though we aren't really very good at this sort of cat and mouse game. We can give our own boys a little credit, though. They aren't really trying to hit us. They shoot well enough to be able to make it look very good. All we really have to worry about is Thurlow and his trained deputy, Trainor.

There, that was nice. The sheriff himself just spotted us and started a pincer movement—fifty yards in back of us. Good old boy. Hope he doesn't get in trouble over us.

At last! If this patch of swampy brush is really as thick as we ESP it we're made, providing the highway troopers of this state don't get too smart and take over the operation. Our sheriff is in charge so far. Lord, if we only weren't so tired!

Anyhow, Lucy brought Thurlow in and we gave him the usual treatment. The only trouble is we overdid it slightly and it scared him. Besides telling him what he had for breakfast we ESPed his wallet and told him its contents and when he reached for it in a sort of stunned reflex action we levitated it into his hand. It was a pretty big mistake in view of the fact that he was one of that bunch that was fairly sensitive mentally, but whom we couldn't read thoroughly. We could telepath only the very surface of his mind. He would have made a wonderful adept with the proper training.

He was awed but shocked and scared, too. It was outside his realm of experience and he was superstitious in spite of his fine education. Some folks don't let learning sink in to open the rusty locks of prejudice and inhibition.

He said things that bared his mind as surely as if we had read him. It wasn't a pretty mind, either. It made us sick physically and the impulses that did come through were deep and angry, giving us a terrific headache and making it hard to concentrate. Later we followed him but still couldn't read him for the anger flashes blotted out his thought stream thoroughly.

To him, what we were doing just couldn't happen in good old 1983. We were dealing in the black arts and he told us as much, refusing to listen to reason in any shape. The fact that everyone has these capabilities latent was altogether lost on him. Our licenses, diplomas and degrees meant less than nothing and the longer he went on the more rabid he got, frothing obscenely about such things as tampering with forces better left alone and man thinking with his brains instead of letting the Prince of Darkness do it for him. Had it not been so serious it would have been almost slapstick. Instead he was tragic.

When he got to the part about us eventually filling the minds of children with our loathsome disease he ran out of expletives and stormed out of the office in a cloud of anger and fright, muttering that we hadn't heard the last of *him*.

Lucy, of course, was heartsick. We didn't have to tell her what the meeting had meant. Nor did we tell her what else we'd ESPed in Thurlow's wallet. She found that out during the rather abortive lesson we tried to give her for she read as we interrupted it (that shows how much off beam we were because we just don't do that) to take a phone call from Casey down at the sheriff's office. Our visitor, Thurlow, was District Judge Thurlow of District Two, a very high man on the law enforcement pole.

Casey was good. He'd listened in while Thurlow was complaining to the sheriff and apparently heard the sheriff read the judge off politely but nonetheless firmly, telling him first how valuable we were to the force when it came to interrogating hard-to-crack suspects and as long as we hadn't committed murder or rape or passed any bum checks there was nothing to be done. Especially since the judge His Honor was out of his district! Fortunately we were in District One over which our mutual friend, Judge Kimball, presides.

Incidentally, Kimball was still under doctor's care at the time due to his latest heart attack. He was getting along quite well but he was old and his days on the bench were pretty well numbered. Casey thought that District One might conceivably have to appoint a new judge to hold them over until election due to the fall court calendar. As it turned out that didn't happen.

Br-r-r! Princess, don't ever let anyone tell you that swamp water can't get cold in summertime. We've got the shakes pretty bad both from our ordeal and from chill. Getting uncomfortably hungry, too. That's what comes of letting an inferior enemy panic you. We certainly haven't acted as though we had better sense. It's just another of those imponderables to chalk up for study.

After Casey's call the air seemed to be cleared and under that driving compulsion which has never left us we went on about the business of trying to succeed with nature since she had succeeded so well with us. The study of the deep processes of the mind eclipsed the next two days and only the terrible jangle of that outmoded telephone brought us to the surface again. It's too bad that we had to converse orally with the great masses of the untrained. It's so slow and they could learn so easily.

It was Casey again, telling us we were needed down at the station. He was apparently calling us on blind orders, for he couldn't tell us what was up. Figuring that we had another prisoner to crack we closed classes and drove down. The sheriff seemed mystified, too, and just slightly troubled. We could read that much off the surface of his mind, but he was upset enough to make the rest of his thoughts a meaningless jumble of impulses. All he knew was that we were wanted in the judge's chambers.

You guessed it, Honey. It was Judge Thurlow filling in for Kimball on an emergency hearing and he figured it was his duty to mankind to give us a little talking to while he was there. After all, the good of the community was his concern now, and he chose to interpret that as the opportunity to place his narrow little views on record. Trainor, the sheriff's deputy faithful only to the judge, because of a favor granted while he served in Thurlow's district, was very busy signing his name to something when we walked into the chambers. It gave us a peculiar feeling to see Thurlow sitting at Kimball's desk. It bore out our theory about a room taking on the personality of its occupant. This room was no longer warm and friendly.

The only thing we could read from Thurlow was a selfrighteous anger and a solemn, nasty vow to fight us to the last ditch—which, incidentally, he has done for that irrigation ditch is the last one we ever wish to occupy. That water was miserably cold.

Three guesses what Trainor was signing. Of all things, a complaint charging us with questionable educational technique! The one thing not covered by license, as Thurlow made haste to confirm through the State House, and by Trainor's complaint, the one way we could legally come into his hands. It was a dainty little frame but unbreakable. Spreading a sweet legal shovel he asked us questions that minutely covered every phase and method of our teaching, then smiled a nasty smile, the while fixing his own signature to another wisp of terribly binding paper. A restraining order.

The words of which forbade us to teach! We were to suspend our life's work or suffer the punishment for contempt of court because of a narrow-minded, righteously wrathful mental prude!

How can you fight something like that? Thurlow was the last and highest branch of authority in the area unless we took it to Supreme Court. For a while we were tempted to do that but on what were we to base a case? Public opinion would throw us out of court if the Supreme Justice didn't.

We talked to the sheriff when we came down and he and his boys were on our side—emotionally. Legally they had to carry out the judge's orders to place us under institutional restraint if we transgressed. In short, we would be tossed in the pokey if we thumbed our noses at the order.

The sheriff's advice was to suspend operations until Supreme Court sat and take it to them. When we asked if he and his staff would be witnesses for us—well, that's water under the oft mentioned bridge. There are some ugly facets of politics that force the men playing them to act as they do. Otherwise we surely wouldn't have been refused. So there we were; no witnesses—no case; because we couldn't bring our pupils into it. It was an uncertain mess at best and we didn't want them to get it in the neck along with us. For the same reason we couldn't involve our former teachers at the university. What poor payment for hours of drudgery to be dragged into a court battle!

So with the sheriff's advice to go into another business ringing in our ears, we came back home to sweat it out and think. It took a while, but the only answer we felt was right under the circumstances was to go underground. That makes it sound like the dark ages, doesn't it, Princess, when knowledge has to hide and creep and skulk instead of flowering under the sun? Our gifts couldn't be let go to waste, not after the preparation and development that went into expanding them into a workable set of psychic senses. We *had* to give Man the benefit of our awakening by waking him in turn.

It's much too bad that we were so sheltered at the university. We might have had some practical experience with the world and its people. We might also have known what to do about this awful hunger that is gradually tearing us down. It's getting to be a serious problem in our untrained condition. The prof's wouldn't even let us play handball for fear of injury so consequently we're nothing but a living cliche, skin and bones. Donald feels it strongly. We shall have to try to buoy each other and go on our combined reserves. Pray that we don't get too weak. It's been almost 24 hours since we've eaten, as there wasn't time for breakfast. Our clothes seem to be drying slightly though it's still cool enough to make it uncomfortable and dangerous. This is the way colds grab you.

We did pretty well in our choice of an underground location—we thought. Our mistake was in overlooking the police trained mind of our bloodhound friend, Trainor. He's a shrewd man and not unintelligent though sadly misguided. How we should like to have him on our side!

In five days of sniffing around he had us located, and in another, he had enough proof of activity to report to Thurlow and come after us with a bench warrant of arrest. It's peculiar that we couldn't stall him or dodge him some way with our much touted IQ, but probably we were still too naive about human relations and most assuredly unversed in the devious twistings of the police mind. After all, though we're twenty-six years old, our experience with people put us in about the three year old class. So you see? Were it to begin all over again the outcome would be different. We would be more practical and worldly. You learn.

There was no sense fighting him, because he had the law enforcement agencies of the whole state in back of him. All he had to do was whisper "Sic 'em" and we were dead. So we went along quietly to see Thurlow and that dear man took a singularly fiendish delight in imposing an impossible fine on us for contempt of court. Our particular transgression wasn't definitively covered by law so neither was the fine. The fact that Thurlow was fining us for teaching methods instead of the contempt charge didn't dawn on us until just yesterday. How completely ignorant can you get?

He gave us a pretty, selfrighteous speech about the good of the community and a judge's place in it, mentioning in passing that everything wasn't covered by law so it was up to the judge to handle matters as he saw fit. That was what he was trained and elected for and that was what he was doing. Nothing personal, understand. As it was, and well he knew it, we couldn't begin to pay the fine so we were informed that we'd have to sit it out in the county jail at the rate of two dollars a day.

The fine was five hundred dollars.

The sheriff almost cried when he found we were to be taking advantage of his hospitality. Very likely the full injustice of the judge's complacent little scheme finally got through to him. At any rate, sympathy or not, we had eight months and ten days to serve with time off possible for good behavior. That's where you found us when you finished your vacation and discovered you were temporarily out of a job.

Donald took quick advantage of a prisoner's rights to telephone Judge Kimball. He was still in bed but sounded fairly strong. His consternation over our new address was touching and real, but we were sadly informed that ethically the whole matter was beyond him. When Thurlow sat in for him in his district, then Thurlow was law and no reversal could be had outside of the due process of that law through a higher court.

He, Kimball, could do nothing until he could get back on the bench. That might be several weeks yet as he wasn't to get out of bed or get excited in any way.

We hung up and had our first look at the familiar cells from the prisoner's viewpoint. The change in outlook was subtle but definite. The walls looked grayer.

Hope we're not boring you with all this, Kitten, but we must tell it to someone and you are closest and dearest to us. You missed out on nearly all our doings after we closed the school so call it a filling-in process. Someone should have the full story although what good it will ever do is debatable. Perhaps at some future time we can do something with it—if we get out of the present jackpot.

Got to move. The state police have taken over the operation and our sheriff is relegated to the role of visiting fireman. It's lamentable that we aren't in his bailiwick. Things might work out better.

These troopers are very efficient. Donald ESPs them folding a cordon around our end of the swamp. All we can do is head through its length now. Trainor is with them. Thurlow has joined them also. We get a tiny jab of pain as we pass over him. That impossible man!

Naturally our pupils fell off, thinking the school completely shut down, until you visited us and were able to pass the word that discreet visits wouldn't go unrewarded. Only a few drifted back for deeper learning and expansion, as you know. One happy thing about the others who were afraid to come back is that they would still make progress, having once been awakened, though it would be infinitely slow and groping. The nucleus that sat with us on those once a week school days grew stronger very rapidly, for knowledge is cumulative and progressive, and they began to realize what they in turn had to do when they were ready. Credit must be given their strength of mind for seeing and accepting such a responsibility with the enthusiasm they showed.

It was too good to last. Trainor's turn at afternoon shift came around and lasted the usual month which gave him plenty of opportunity to watch us like a hawk. He did. We were cautious but we couldn't know what he was watching for, because he didn't know either. He found out one afternoon. Visitors just don't come around and merely sit—staring at each other or the walls.

We learned another lesson from that: men with as much training as he had don't always consciously think things out with their surface minds. Their reactions became instinctive and as such, untraceable by the most adept telepath. We knew he was there to spy but that's about all.

The net result was a direct order from Thurlow cutting off not only all visitors, but as Trainor gleefully advised us, cancelling all accrued days off for good behavior. That's five days a month in this state and it was almost unbearable. The thorough injustice of the whole affair was beginning to gall mightily, getting under our rather thin skin in many places.

What seemed the final crushing blow was the news that filtered in to us from Judge Kimball's court reporter. He'd taken word to the sick man about our latest loving treatment by Thurlow and it angered Kimball enough to make him get out of bed—too soon. He died on the floor of his bedroom. So, not only do we lose a dear friend, but also any chance of his assistance. Thurlow would now sit for District One until election time. That put us entirely on our own resources.

After much deliberation, we decided to give in and go back to the university when our sentence was up and take advantage of its sheltering walls for our teaching. We would be absorbed into the faculty and soon all this unpleasantness would pass over.

How we passed the time until our release is unimportant to anyone but us. During the remaining months, we delved farther and farther into the mind and gained a much deeper insight into the workings of these gifts we had. Man could be so powerful and work so much for his own good—if he could only be made to realize the potential in his mind! He could even be happy.

The bright day came at last, and we walked out of our cell free to begin again. It was raining a gray rain outside, but to us the weather had never looked brighter. As we reached for the sheriff's phone to call the university, Trainor sidled up and laid a scrap of paper on the desk. A glance was enough to make us hang up on the uncompleted call.

It was another restraining order.

After that we tried to find work on the outside, but it was a sorry failure. The curse of being different is a mighty one indeed. No one seemed to care that we had feelings the same as others and that we could get just as hungry and thirsty without funds to buy.

Ahh! There it is again. Those words. Hunger and thirst. As if we needed a reminder. Donald is getting weaker in perception. He has always been the first to feel such things and we've never been able to trace the reason. We certainly have no—

---

*I interject at this point, for telepathic contact with them broke unexplainably. I prayed for their safety for I suddenly knew what it would mean to lose them. What a drab, dreary, bigoted world it would be without them to teach us and help us.*

---

God, that was a bad half hour, Puss. These troopers are so well trained that they're more telepathically dead than you can imagine. First, Donald was so weak he let one of them sneak up close enough for a quick rifle shot. It missed, but of course it told exactly where we were. Donald exerted himself and ESPed locations, finding that we had enough time to work on the trooper if we hurried. Normally we'd be no match for him but desperation can work wonders. We resorted to a base form of trickery by affecting to surrender to him. When he came up to put the cuffs on us, we played dirtier by offering him a knee that will keep him from attending his wife for a few days. Rotten trick, but we couldn't afford to let him get his hands on us or it would have been all finished. That makes another count against us. We left his rifle out of reach and ran.

Fortunately the others milled around for a precious minute or two when they found him, giving us still more time. Before they got moving again, we broke cover and made it across a county road into a farmer's barn where we burrowed into the hay. We'll stay here a while to rest. Not being the athletic type we sure need it.

To go back, our small supply of money was running dangerously low in spite of miserly budgeting. We didn't know what to do outside of robbing a bank to get more. Then it happened.

We were browsing through the library one day, when Donald ESPed a stack of returned books not yet filed hoping to turn up something new. The stack was mixed, holding such things as a treatise on grinding optical lenses, a copy of "Gone With the Wind", a couple of western novels, a thin edition of "The Purloined Letter" and several volumes for the home craftsman. Evidently some newlyweds were doing things to their well mortgaged dream house.

On the way home, Donald's idea burst in on both of us like some monstrous flashbulb. With our minds being so perfectly tuned through constant work during the years, what one ESPed the telepath had immediately and what one telepathed the ESPer received at once. It was a fine working agreement and became as habitual as breathing. Donald's idea was beautiful for all that it was lifted from another man. Its application was what burnished it to that bright luster of originality.

We would go to work in a carnival! If a man could hide a letter in an open letter rack, where better could we be hidden but in a carnival? It was wonderful.

We had no trouble getting into one. The owner took one look at what we could do and told us the answer mentally by wondering how little he could offer and still get us. It gave us a certain bargaining point but at our stage of the game all we wanted was in. The thought crossed our minds that we might be lowering our station in life but we were past caring.

And of course we found out how wrong we were, that "station in life" is just a point of view. To outsiders carnies are a hard lot, interested in nothing but the quickest way to part the suckers from a dollar. Well, they *were* hard, to outsiders, but to those inside there is a difference. We found some mighty fine people and some very fertile minds.

We enjoyed the first real security we'd known for a long time. We found friendship and a certain amount of fame as moneymakers for the show. We got a raise after working on the boss for a while. Best of all we lost ourselves in the bustle of the show.

Shortly after our admission into the ranks of the carnies, we felt safe enough to put out feelers (we were out of the state by then), mental this time, prodding small ideas into the best minds, giving them the urge to ask us questions of a leading nature and so eventually we began another class in telepathy, ESP, and their related subjects. As we traveled from state to state we picked up new pupils from other shows and lost others to the same shows, but the running count was about twenty most of the time.

We had to be so very careful in our selections for fear of a repetition of our former mishaps, but it went well. We made no mistakes and turned out some fine pupils, one in particular. He progressed fast enough in the short time we had him to become acutely adept, and when we told him he was ready to teach he accepted it by leaving the carnival to settle down with a home and wife. It was good to see the fruit of our work being put into practice.

Next season, we found that in the first pass across the country we were booked for the north end of our home state. For the first time in nearly two years we would be on almost familiar ground.

You know what happened then, Baby. You ought to. You were the one we contacted. Telepathy *is* a lot better than a telephone, isn't it?

What you might not know is that our contact with you was another step in this whole sickening drama. How were we to suspect that the train ticket agent was one of those tenacious, bespectacled fellows who doggedly chewed on an idea until it made sense to him? Who would know that he was one of those spiteful, small people who enjoyed doing his civic duty as he saw it?

He wondered why so many people were taking the same train on the same day to the same place, when it had never happened before. People just don't travel three hundred miles to take in a one horse carnival.

Being a small town he knew most of the folks by name—or at least by sight—and he recalled that you, sweet, were once our secretary.

Imagine the excitement he felt at having such a momentous thing happen in his dull and uneventful life. How best to savour the taste of it? Why, call the sheriff, naturally. Oh, it must have been delicious. Let's hope he enjoys the memory.

With our luck it was out of the question to have anyone but Trainor answer the phone—and swing into high gear. Apparently Judge Thurlow had run for District One during the election and made it, giving up his own stamping grounds for some reason. It hardly seems possible that he'd do it just on the hope that we might decide to come home and set up shop. No man could be that vindictive, could he? Or are we still much too naive to be allowed out without a keeper? Who knows?

We do know that the group was followed by Trainor and another man at Thurlow's orders; and when they saw all of you meet at a certain tent in back of the midway all they had to do was sneak close enough to hear that there was exactly nothing going on! We were all so excited at seeing each other that their presence went unnoticed. Besides, what need to exercise caution when there wasn't an unfriendly face within miles?

When Trainor made his telephone call to get the permission to arrest us on the strength of another bench warrant Thurlow prepared in a hurry, his emotions penetrated our little circle; but not soon enough for everyone to get out safely. It all happened so suddenly that our lifelong control snapped. The persecution was so sneaking and so needless!

It didn't take long to dispose of the two deputies. Desperation again and thick anger. We lost no time in trussing them solidly and leaving them unconscious. After it was over, we realized what a deadly game it had suddenly become. We were in deep trouble again—deeper than any that had gone before. And we needed time, lots of it.

Take our word for it, Kitten, and stay underground during any time you and the others may teach. It's your duty to use care, because you certainly won't be able to advance your state of learning or help others while under detention. Keep in touch with the others. Your ranks will fill, if you can succeed undetected until it's time to come into the open.

Don't get into our fix; don't be forced into breaking the law. We didn't break it by teaching supposedly Satanic courses but by ignoring the restraining order, then by beating up the police and running. Running wasn't too bad in itself, but it made it tougher when in our shocked haste we took a car that didn't belong to us. Then, too, we shouldn't have taken it across the state line. That made it a federal offense. Even if the troopers get us, we shall first be guests of the FBI. Sweet mess, isn't it?

Lordy, this hay is dry. It's sweet smelling and comfortable lying here but it's dry and dusty. It'll be too bad if nature gives us away through a tickling nose. We can do without her tricks now.

Donald has just ESPed a water trough in back of the barn. We must take a chance on it. This raging thirst is as crippling as the lack of food.

We drove in a huge circle and left the car well before morning; continuing on foot in the general direction of our friend who had left the carnival to teach. It was our hope to be able to stay there until things cooled down.

We finally made it, tired and hungry, and got the welcome we expected. He was overjoyed to see us. You'll never know how cosy and warm that house felt or how utterly *good* was the smell of baking bread. His wife is a jewel.

We received a jolt the next morning before breakfast. The neighbor's little girl came bursting into the house in what apparently was her normal fashion while we were teaching a small class that our friend had collected. She was extraordinarily sensitive and our combined minds made a terrific impact on her perception before we could control it.

Her eyes opened and she was all for broadcasting to every child in the block, but Donald got us through a sticky moment. He made it her own personal secret in a way that only children can appreciate and then showed her one of the simpler tricks of ESP. She grasped it at once for children are extraordinarily susceptible to instruction. Their minds haven't had the chance to get cluttered by inhibitions and conventional thoughts. She was wide-eyedly delighted and promised her cross-my-heart promise that no one would ever know about us.

But of course, they did. Parents being what they are, it was foolish to assume that an untrained child could keep the signs of her adventure from them. The signs pointed to a story and it didn't take them long to pry it out of her. It wasn't the girl's fault. The adult odds were against her.

They poked and prodded at her for the cause of her overly bright eyes and animated spirit, until the poor child was overwrought and blurted out the details of her immense find. The mother was at once sympathetic to her and us, bless her, but not so the father. They both knew she wasn't imagining it because of the stories they'd heard of us over the years and the father blew up. We could sense the whole tableau telepathically, dreading the outcome, knowing what it must be.

The father stormed about the house crying death and destruction on us, while the mother tried to get him to listen to reason. He was mentally incapable of doing it. He, like so many of the others, was terribly frightened at the unknown, fearsome thing in their midst. It was unthinkable that we should stay free of captivity when there were places for people like us! We shouldn't be allowed to mingle with normal, decent folks. The upshot was a long distance, collect phone call to the judge who doubtless accepted the charges quite happily.

We couldn't stay, so we turned to run once more.

That's about all there is, Princess. We've run until we can hardly run any more. We're weak and hungry and sickened by the hatred and stupid, active resistance surrounding us. We don't blame the police. They're merely doing what they are paid to do.

Donald has ESPed them filtering through the swamp in a wide semicircle and a few thoughts are leaking through the jumble of shouted orders and mixed impulses. Trainor and the judge are right with them. He seems to be talking earnestly to Trainor but his hatred and anger blot everything out—we can get nothing from him. Donald is getting weaker, but we must stir to get water and try to leave before they see this barn.

---

*Here the narrative broke once more for more than an hour, leaving me in an agonized, hopeless suspense, knowing there was no way to help them. Occasionally I sensed a faint stirring in my mind as though they were trying to get through to me and once a deep stab of sorrow amounting almost to pain. It was getting quite late in the evening before they came through once more, weakly but still clearly and coherently.*

---

It's hard to concentrate. The ambulance is jerking and bounding along and the pain is frightful. Looking back, there was no other way for it to end. They were too many and too dedicated, while we were only us and on the run, not even on the defensive.

Our physical weakness became painfully apparent when we cautiously ventured out back to find the water trough, drank, and stumbled away from our pursuers for a quarter of a mile right into the hands of six waiting state policemen. We'd been so intent on the men in the swamp, so blanketed by Thurlow's hate, and so tired that we didn't sense the danger from another direction in the form of a flanking movement. The operation was the end for us. They all had drawn weapons, but when they saw our sad state they rather sheepishly put them away and took us almost gently in hand.

We're getting weaker. Unconsciousness is near again. Would that we could have stayed with them!

Instead, one picked up a walkie-talkie and called in our capture. Even in the turmoil of the moment we could pick up flashes of amazed, frightened and curious thoughts as many of them saw us for the first time. Funny how the mind will act at times of stress, making one an observer of one's own actions, so to speak. Another phase opened for study!

Thurlow thanked the state men brusquely and said he and his deputies would take over, airily ignoring extradition procedure. The police chief and our sheriff were dubious about the course events were taking, but didn't want trouble so they offered no active resistance.

We were too tired to care any more. That was our third mistake, to lose our alertness completely. Had we been quick enough—but no, we couldn't have avoided it. The old story of trained men reacting without conscious thought.

Apparently in accordance with previous instruction, Trainor and his helper began jostling us viciously but expertly, making it appear as though we were trying to escape. Before we realized our danger, we heard a cry of warning from the sheriff and a vindictive shout from Thurlow. It still rings in our ears.

"Do your duty, Trainor. They're escaping!"

Trainor's reflexes jarred him into action and it was over for us almost before it began. It hurt then, but the pain is worse now and total blackness is closing in once more. Fighting it off gets increasingly difficult, alone as I am.

You see, Donald has just died, quietly. He's escaped them, but that leaves the fight to me. It won't last long. The load is too much for one alone. The one bright feature is the fact that our work was begun. Stay with it, darling, and carry on for us—please know that you had all our love.

Goodbye, Princess.

---

*Almost exactly one minute later they arrived at the hospital. I was so numb with grief and sorrow that I didn't withdraw contact, hoping against hope that they, he, would transmit once more. He did, unconsciously. Seconds later the words of two interns drifted through his open mind to mine.*

---

"One D. O. A., one dying fast. My God, Rex, why couldn't they leave the poor devils alone? Why couldn't they—"

Rex sounded bitter. "You know the answer to that, Tom. They were different so they didn't belong."

Milton Keynes UK
Ingram Content Group UK Ltd.
UKHW010857211223
434780UK00006B/408